A SENSE OF BELONGING:

SHOULD I MAINSTREAM MY CHILD?

Bev Chambers

NAE

First published 2001
© New Africa Books (Pty) Ltd
PO Box 23317, Claremont 7735
South Africa

New Africa Education (NAE) is an imprint of New Africa Books (Pty) Ltd.

ISBN: 1-919876-05-7

Editing: Moeneba Slamang
Layout and design: Jenny Wheeldon
Photographs: Bev Chambers (cover, 29, 31); Gill Lanham (cover, 22); Carol Smith (15)
Cover design: Jenny Wheeldon

Every effort has been made to trace copyright holders. Should any infringements have
occured, please inform the publisher who will correct these in the event of a reprint.

Printed and bound in the Republic of South Africa by Formeset Printers
Cape (Pty) Ltd.

With special thanks to Jess who was my inspiration and to Carol who was my support and encouragement. Thanks also to all those who shared their time and thoughts on inclusion with me, and to Kalk Bay Primary, Beckford Primary School and Chameleon Pre-school and Educare Centre for allowing us to photograph there.

CONTENTS

CHAPTER 1
INTRODUCTION

We all want the best for our children. Exactly what that is, is a constant dilemma for any parent, but more so for parents of children with disabilities. From the early days of diagnosis, parents are either given no help or information, or are bombarded with opinions from all sources. The confusion of the unknown and the unexpected situation complicates decision making, and to parents of children with disabilities there often seems to be no alternative but to accept the course of action the professionals propose – medically or educationally. However, it should always be remembered that the professionals are offering not indisputable facts, but rather opinions based on their field of study and their experience. Trained professionals may provide advice that does not necessarily co-incide with what is best for your child. Every child is an individual, and therefore the same input may produce varied outcomes in different children.

When my daughter, Jessica, was first diagnosed, the doctor and the physiotherapist gave assessments that, now with experience, I realise were only their opinions. At the time, I perceived their assessments as factual truths, which plunged me into a state of despair. Dr M told me: "this child will never sit or walk or go to a normal school, and there is concern about her ability to communicate". She was 11 months old then. Now, aged 8, she speaks wonderfully, she sits unsupported, she reads fluently and she goes to a mainstream school. She walks with the support of a frame and is determined to prove Dr M wrong by walking independently. All of these skills have been acquired through hard work and perseverance, and I am quite sure that if we had followed the advice of Dr M and placed her in the school that was suggested, Jessica would never have achieved what she has, but rather merely have met the doctors' expectations of her.

As parents, we need to be provided with a spectrum of alternatives so that we can make informed choices. We need to be shown the implications of the various choices. Most of all, like any parent, we need to be respected and empowered in our roles as parents so that we can be effective allies to our children.

> We need to get away from the attitude that only professionals know what is best for people with disabilities. I see it every day from government employees, providers and parents of adults with disabilities. Adults with disabilities and families of children with disabilities need to be able to choose for themselves.
> (Martin – paediatric doctor)

The options for education are often presented as falling into one of two categories – mainstream school or special school, but it is never as simple as that. What is involved in each of these choices? What are the expected outcomes for the child as an individual? Why are there special schools? Are mainstream schools always inclusive? Will the school we choose be able to meet our child's needs? These are all questions that parents ask and try to find answers to.

It is through my daughter that I have been given the opportunity to question these issues for myself and to explore some of the avenues that were open to us. Jessica has been very involved in my work on this book, and here she introduces herself and shares her story.

<u>My move to mainstream</u>

I am 8 years old and I go to Beckford school. I have got a quadruplegic disability. That is really in my two legs and in my left hand but not in my right hand because I use that hand well. I can move around on the floor on my own but at scool I have to use my electric wheelchair. the sort of help I need is help with going to the toilet, help with getting my dinner and also help with speed with writing.

I left Horton Lodge school in July 1998 so that was just before the summer holidays and i started at beckford school in late september because I couldn't get a place till then. For the first term at beckford i only did half day at school because i would do physical stuff at home instead of at school.

My favorite thing about beckford is that we actually have a proper playground and they have an exsplorers challenge with lots of things to climb on.

One lucky escape from horton was task series (thats where you do lots of physical exercises to sit and walk.) but I miss horse riding and all of my friends. Some of my new friends are called Shannon Dixon, hannah Adu-baah, Cherise Mir, Colin Danskin and Samantha Ward.

Two things I like best are P.E. and show and tell. The one thing I dont like is school dinner so I dont have it anymore. I have pack lunch instead with my friends Shannon and cherise.

CHAPTER 2
WHAT IS INCLUSION?

Defining the terminology

There is often confusion around some of the terms that are used for mainstream and special education, and in the way that each of these is used. Here is a description of how most people use them and how they are used in this book.

A *mainstream school* is a regular school that caters for the needs of ordinary children. Traditionally, all children attend mainstream school unless there is a reason for placing them in a school for specific learning disabilities.

A *special school* is a school that is set up to cater for the needs of a specific group of children such as those who have motor disorders or hearing or visual impairments. Many of these schools have had to broaden the criteria of the type of children that they accept because often there is overlap in the needs of children. For example, an autistic child may also have co-ordination difficulties; or a child with cerebral palsy may be mobile but have learning difficulties; while another may not be able to walk, but have no additional needs that are different from other children in mainstream schools.

A *special class* may be one class within a mainstream school that caters for the needs of children with disabilities.

A *special needs teacher* is one who has been trained to help children access and understand the curriculum more easily.

A *special needs co-ordinator* is the person in the school in charge of the special needs children, often a special needs teacher.

A *learning support facilitator* assists a child with physical transfers and educational or physical needs in the classroom or playground.

Mainstreaming is the placement of all children in "regular" classrooms that are in "regular" schools.

Inclusion refers to the opportunity for every child to participate in and benefit from all activities within the mainstream school system.

The inclusion movement

School is often the first move away from the extended family and is therefore an important link for a child to the big world outside. It should be a place that nurtures and sustains a child's development. It should continue the growth of a child's self-awareness, encouraging a healthy and positive self-image. Growing up in an environment that is accepting and inclusive gives any child the freedom to develop positive self-esteem. The confidence that this breeds will win the greater part of the battle for children with disabilities. With this inner strength, children are more likely to fulfil their potential and overcome their specific problems.

> The greatest barrier to achievement is confidence. If confidence levels are high and self-esteem is good, all sorts of limits can be pushed and great things can happen. With praise and encouragement, a child can reach full potential, often beyond all hopes and expectations.
>
> *(Pamela – principal of a mainstream school)*

Children with disabilities have to overcome their individual problems, as well as battle against other people's perceptions of them. The supporters of inclusion argue that by removing children with disabilities from their peer groups, we deny non-disabled children the opportunity to learn about, experience and become aware of disability. Therefore we also lose the chance to change the perceptions that lock people with disabilities into certain boxes and oppress them. Every child with a difference or a disability that is included in a mainstream school helps to challenge stereotypes and build awareness. Challenging negative perceptions is empowering for all children – those with disabilities as well as their able-bodied peers.

INCLUSIVE EDUCATION IS A HUMAN RIGHT, IT'S GOOD EDUCATION AND IT MAKES GOOD SOCIAL SENSE.

TEN REASONS FOR INCLUSION

Human rights

1. All children have the right to learn together.

2. Children should not be devalued or discriminated against by being excluded or sent away because of their disability or learning difficulty.

3. Disabled adults, describing themselves as special school survivors, are demanding an end to segregation.

4. There are no legitimate reasons to separate children for their education. Children belong together – with advantages and benefits for everyone. They do not need to be protected from each other.

Good education

5. Research shows children do better, academically and socially, in integrated settings.

6. There is no teaching or care in a segregated school which cannot take place in an ordinary school.

7. Given commitment and support, inclusive education is a more efficient use of education resources.

Good social sense

8. Segregation teaches children to be fearful and ignorant, and breeds prejudice.

9. All children need an education that will help them develop relationships and prepare them for life in the mainstream.

10. Only inclusion has the potential to reduce fear and to build friendship, respect and understanding.

Prepared by the Centre for Studies on Inclusive Education (CSIE), United Kingdom

We learn prejudice, we are not born with it. Children need to be provided with accurate information about disabilities and other differences. They need opportunities to learn to challenge stereotyping and they need to be taught to handle name calling, physical barriers and attitudes. In an environment that strives to break down stereotypes by providing factual information, children will be able to recognise and challenge bias and prejudice. They will see that differences contribute towards positive learning experiences.

Today, more than ever before, there is an emphasis on *celebrating* differences, rather than highlighting difference as a negative issue. Children with disabilities provide the opportunity for celebration of difference, and so to remove them from a mainstream school is an impoverishing loss, and a missed opportunity for everyone's personal growth. It is also a human rights issue, and contradicts any idea of civil liberties. Children have the right to be educated alongside their peers.

> The friendships that the learners with special needs develop in school carry through after school as well ... I think that's because everyone in the classroom is seen as belonging. They see each other as different, but they celebrate the differences rather than focus on them in a negative way.
>
> *(Christina – teacher in a mainstream school)*

All children deserve to be valued and treated as individuals within their broader group of peers. It is important for all of our children to be accepted for who they are, instead of by the labels that categorise them. A sense of belonging is what makes an individual flourish. If all children are allowed to remain within their peer groups, as part of their own communities, there is a natural learning experience that comes from varied exposure. The richness of experience will be great – for both the individual and the group.

> Segregated schools perpetuate the perceptions that people have about disability. They deny the rest of society the opportunity of learning – learning that disability is like any difference. That's all it is – different.
>
> *(Julie – parent)*

Inclusive education is gradually becoming a reality. In many countries, schools are legally required to accept all children and provide for their special needs. While on paper things have improved, there are loopholes, which often means that the reality does not always match the law. However, to varying degrees, inclusive practices are being implemented, for example, some mainstream and special schools are working together, learning support facilitators are being assigned to mainstream schools, and training for teachers to help them work with children with special needs is being made available as these children are integrated into mainstream settings.

Inclusive education has taken many different forms in different countries around the world. This has ranged from integrating all children into the mainstream, regardless of the severity of disabilities, to more gradual approaches where there is still access to special schooling but where mainstreaming is an option.

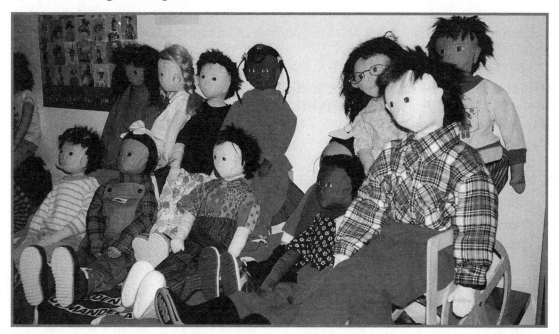

Persona dolls are used with young children to help develop empathy, respect for difference and a sense of fairness

In the United Kingdom, the Warnock Commission and Report led to the 1981 Education Act. Prior to this, children with special needs were catered for at the special schools in the area in which they lived, even if the disability that the school was directed at was not the same as the disability of the child. Of course, because children's needs often varied from the focus of the available special school, children did not always receive the most appropriate education. Things changed with the implementation of the 1981 Education Act. The starting point became the child and his or her needs, rather than what provision was available. An assessment of the child as an individual clarified what specific needs there might be and how best to meet them. As a result of this approach and the support of laws about access to schools and the curriculum, education in mainstream schools became available to more and more children with disabilities.

> The road to an inclusive school is a process, not a state.
>
> *(James – special needs co-ordinator in a mainstream school)*

In the United States of America, the Individuals with Disabilities Act, formerly known as Public Law 94–142, was passed in 1975 and reauthorised in 1990. This law mandates that all children receive free, appropriate public education regardless of the level or severity of their disability. Funds are provided to assist states in the education of children with disabilities, and states are required to make sure that these children receive an individualised education programme based on their unique needs in the least restrictive environment possible.

At an international conference on inclusive education in Spain in 1994, the United Nations Educational, Scientific and Cultural Organisation (UNESCO) adopted the Salamanca Statement, which now forms the basis for their work in special needs education. This document states that:

❖ every child has a fundamental right to education and must be given the opportunity to achieve and maintain an acceptable level of learning

❖ every child has unique characteristics, interests, abilities and learning needs

❖ education systems should be designed, and educational programmes implemented to take into account the wide diversity of these characteristics and needs

❖ those with special education needs must have access to regular schools which should accommodate them within a child-centred pedagogy capable of meeting these needs

❖ regular schools with this inclusive orientation are the most effective means of combating discriminatory attitudes, creating welcoming communities, building an inclusive society and achieving education for all; moreover, they provide an effective education to the majority of children and improve the efficiency and ultimately the cost effectiveness of the education system

Current policy and practice in South Africa

As a result of apartheid policies, the provision of schooling for children with disabilities in the past was segregated and diverse. Those who were classified as "white" were educated in special schools or in special classes. There was some provision in special schools for children classified "coloured" and "Indian", but less than that provided for "white" children. For children classified "black", there was virtually no provision, so some children were mainstreamed by default, but many were kept at home – not through choice, but simply because there was no alternative schooling available for them.

The South African Schools Act of 1996 directs that all children should have access to learning and to equal opportunities in education. Where necessary, they should be given support and state resources should be provided to ensure this. Schools may not refuse access to children with special needs, and parents have the right to choose where they want their children placed.

A policy on special needs education in South Africa is still in development and will draw on the findings of the National Commission on Special Needs in Education and Training (NCSNET) and the National Committee for Education Support Services (NCESS), who have investigated and made proposals on all levels and aspects of education. In their 1997 report, they promote "education for all with the development of inclusive and supportive centres of learning that enable all learners to participate actively in the education process so that they can develop and extend their potential and participate as equal members of society". To achieve this, they propose the following principles:

- ❖ acceptance of principles and values contained in the Constitution and the White Papers on education and training
- ❖ human rights and social justice for all learners
- ❖ participation and social integration
- ❖ equal access to a single, inclusive education system
- ❖ access to the curriculum
- ❖ equity and redress
- ❖ community responsiveness
- ❖ cost-effectiveness

In South Africa, despite moves towards inclusion practices existing on paper, they are not translated into practice equally in all parts of the country, for example, only some provincial education departments have appointed learning support facilitators to support schools that are practising inclusion. The moves are small and vary from area to area, with the whole process being in an embryonic phase.

The introduction of inclusive education has been met with all sorts of barriers. However, as a mainstream school principal once said to me: "it only takes one brave parent to open the doors for

> Michael was the first child with no independent mobility to go to his school. It was a four-storey building and as he progressed through the school, he moved upstairs. For his first four years there, there was no lift and I had to carry him up and down each day. Fortunately we lived close enough to school for me to go to school at lunch break to bring him down. Eventually we got a lift put in and now there are a number of other children there who use it.
>
> *(Alison – parent)*

Jennifer was the first child with hearing problems to go to her school. She only has 30% hearing in one ear, and 40% in the other, so the impairment is quite profound. She has hearing aids and the teacher was wonderful at learning to use them and building awareness with the other children. Once a week there is support from a teacher from the hearing unit at our local hospital, and the class teacher really took that opportunity to learn skills and put them into practice. I felt so lucky that we had such an easy start, and that laid the grounds for the rest of the school. It will be interesting to see what happens when she goes to secondary school.

(Kirsty – parent)

others ...". There are many success stories about the first child with a disability who joined a mainstream school. The reality is, though, that although these children may pave the way for other children to follow, it can be draining for their parents to be constantly fighting for change within schools.

CHAPTER 3
THE DEBATE – MAINSTREAM OR SPECIAL SCHOOL?

Historically, special schools have been developed according to and dominated by medical rather than educational perspectives. When a disability is first diagnosed, parents are often given a list of things that the child won't be able to do, followed by the doctor's opinion of how best to treat this case. With the assumption that disability is caused by a physical or mental problem, this becomes the focus, and with the medical professionals' involvement, the school becomes the place to fix the disability and cure the patient.

The issues are complex, though. It is not just a question of "mainstream versus special school", but rather the implications of either choice. We need to look at the role that special schools actually play. Are they set up for the benefit of the individual, or are they a hang-over from the past when society at large could not bear to deal with the imperfection that disability represents? Is there a way to include children with disabilities in the larger community while still using the provision of special schools? Or do we mainstream all children and then deal with the frustrations that arise in the hopes that one day there will be a smooth flow? How much choice do we give our children? Do we constantly reassess and possibly change direction?

What about the goals of inclusion? Are they to mainstream every child regardless of their disability? Are they to allow every child to develop his or her full potential, to participate in the activities that other children enjoy, and to experience a rich life? It is no use just including children on the periphery. To be on the sideline in a mainstream classroom can be more exclusionary than to be in a special school where children theoretically get more individualised attention. It is also no use putting children into a mainstream environment if they are then just being whisked out for individual tutoring, physiotherapy sessions and the like, and not really enjoying a fully inclusive school day.

Inclusion and mainstreaming may not necessarily be the same thing. Mainstreaming is the placement of children in "regular" classrooms. Inclusion is ensuring that every child is able to participate in and benefit from all activities, with the same opportunities as children without disabilities. So mainstreaming alone does not ensure an experience of inclusive education. However, in order for inclusion to occur, mainstreaming must be a reality.

Nicky is a child with visual impairments. While studying the history and painting style of a particular artist, the teacher took the class to an art gallery, where they heard about the artist's life and looked at some of his paintings. Did Nicky receive the same education as the rest of her mainstream peers? Was she included?

Special schools

In special schools, class sizes are smaller and there is a high staff–pupil ratio, and so the individual attention children receive is usually greater. Also there are likely to be small activity groups, enabling each child to get more participation time. A further consideration is that of facilities and equipment. If a special school is geared towards providing for children with specific needs, then it is likely to have appropriate equipment. In theory, in a special school, children receive appropriate, individualised attention more of the time.

Funding is one of the aspects that has maintained the special school system. To have physiotherapists, speech and occupational therapists in one place seeing to the needs of many individuals is easier and less costly for the state than having such therapists visit a number of schools where perhaps only one child in a school needs attention.

Special schooling may also seem less costly for parents than mainstreaming – financially and time-wise. For parents, special schooling may seem preferable to doing the constant therapy run after school hours, as would most likely be the case in mainstreaming. Aside from the added costs involved for these out-of-school therapies, additional strain is placed on parents in terms of the time it takes to manage the therapy runs. So, for many, special schooling is a very real consideration, and may often seem to be

> Until I was seven I went to my local mainstream school where I was totally included and did well in all my subjects. Two years ago I moved to a "deaf" unit that is attached to a mainstream school. I knew that I would miss my friends and I didn't like the idea of being in a special school. But one thing is different. I feel "less deaf" now that I am here. In the mainstream school, I was always different because of my deafness and it was talked about – not in a bad way. But here I am the same as everyone else, and my deafness isn't such an issue.
>
> *(Matthew – aged 9)*

> Samantha would not be able to cope on her own at a mainstream school – she would have to have a facilitator and that would be privately funded, so it's not an option at the moment. Also I am pleased that she is with other disabled kids as she is then not the only child who is different. I think that if there were other disabled kids at the mainstream school, that point wouldn't apply. Initially I was dead against Samantha attending a special needs school. She was going to be mainstreamed no matter what. I now believe that there is a place for special needs schools especially in the early years.
>
> *(Bridget – parent)*

the only alternative when weighed against the physical, financial and emotional exhaustion that could go along with mainstream schooling.

Early integration

So much at the time of diagnosis depends on the attitudes of the doctor or therapist or the clinic staff. Are they willing to give suggestions and ideas for treatment in the mainstream environment? Do they see your child as an individual? Are they recognising that you are the parent, valuing your opinions and needs, and realising that you are your child's greatest ally? Do they believe that your family and your child should be an integrated part of the society you live in?

> One of the things that has been so difficult since Jessica moved from special school to mainstream, is seeing to all of her additional needs. In the special school, her physio, OT, speech, swimming and horse-riding were all part of the programme. The physio also took care of all of her equipment needs – her wheelchair, bicycle, splints and seating were all constantly checked and monitored. Now that is *all* up to me. At times it is a logistical nightmare.
>
> *(Bev – parent)*

Diagnosis and intervention at an early stage are crucial in order to maximise the potential of the child. As for any child, one with disabilities needs input to develop, to play, to communicate, to learn about the environment and to build relationships. It is important for children to attend age-appropriate playgroups in order to learn skills. Whether these skills are social, cognitive or physical, will depend on the child, but there is no doubt that children will benefit from maximum input at an early stage.

Children acquire and learn so much from one another, just by spending time together. They learn by example and model the actions and behaviour of other children. Physical, social, language and cognitive skills are incorporated into children's games, making them wonderful learning opportunities. For a child with developmental delays, a group of children at play can be a powerful teaching tool.

Peer expectations have an influential effect on the behaviour of children. Through their play, children set up situations for one another to learn and develop. They watch and observe each other, learn what is appropriate or acceptable within the group, and they take risks, learn to problem-solve and rise to the challenges of other children. Children motivate each other in a way that adults are unable to do, and their innate curiosity can spark off a determination to reach all sorts of limits.

> I think that the most important thing is age-appropriate peers as role models. Children learn so much from one another and they live up to peer expectation.
>
> *(Christina – teacher in a mainstream school)*

Young children participating in a creative movement activity at an inclusive pre-school

> One afternoon, getting ready for swimming with an able-bodied friend gave far more motivation to learn to pull off socks than many physiotherapy sessions had done.
>
> *(Bev – parent)*

Of course, your child may require medical intervention as well at this early age. However, many of the skills that your child will be focusing on in therapy sessions can be implemented in playgroup or other mainstream activities. Practising them in this way with other children will make them more fun and your child is likely to learn and progress happily.

As with all parents, if you have a child with a disability, you will need help and support. Playgroups for children can be an advantage for parents as well. There is the immeasurable emotional support that comes through friendship with other parents, which can be uplifting to anyone who is struggling with a child. This support can be found in any type of group – playgroups, swimming lessons or storytime at the library. It does not have to be isolated to a specific group for children with disabilities.

Playgroups that enable children to learn skills also benefit parents in another way. Just as children learn from their peers, so do we as parents. We learn parenting methods and different ways to handle our children, and we also gain an awareness of child development. In this way, we have a chance to acquire ways to help our children's learning to continue at home.

Mainstreaming

Historically, the focus given to disability was based on "fixing" the child – often in an excluded setting away from mainstream society. Of course, developing the child's potential and allowing the child to get more out of life is to be encouraged. However, we need to ask where the best place is to do this – in a special school or in a mainstream environment.

> I was head of department at a special school for years and we helped many children move to mainstream. I found that the biggest dilemma for parents was whether to keep their children in the specialist environment with intensive therapy, or to include them in the big wide world where they may get less "expertise" but more of a "normal" life.
>
> *(Sheena – teacher in a special school)*

While there are numerous advantages for the child in mainstreaming, we need to be aware that stereotypes exist in mainstream society, and that these need constant challenging. The society we live in has a culture of "ableism", which the media and advertising promote. As ableism is promoted, it is done at the expense of people with disabilities, and great strain is placed on professionals and parents to keep fighting the marginalisation that occurs. Parents need to take every opportunity to break down the stereotypes and to create awareness, and at the same time, we need to give our children the greatest chance of fulfilling their potential. We need to constantly monitor our children's progress and assess their changing needs and how these needs are being met by the school they attend.

Jacqui, a social worker, elaborates: "The idea that children are placed out of the mainstream school system and into a special school environment because of their disabilities, reinforces the notion that they should be kept separate and that they are not good enough. To see a group of youngsters out on an excursion with their various carers, does nothing to dispel these attitudes. It all becomes a self-fulfilling cycle, as so many children who have spent large parts of their lives in special schools, often as residents, become institutionalised. They do not have the same opportunities to learn to make decisions, to learn to negotiate, to succeed and to fail, or to just manage the rough and tumble of life. Their lives are ruled by the school bell. How many families manage the rigid routines or times that happen in institutions? The telephone rings, there is an unexpected visitor, the milk runs out. In an institution, these are not run-of-the-mill occurrences – but they *are* part of real life."

In order to give children with disabilities positive messages around their roles in society, we need to give them a valued place in mainstream life. We sometimes tend to underestimate the roles that others' perceptions and attitudes play in our lives, in terms of the negative or positive perceptions we

I've worked in a variety of different situations with learners with special needs, and I really believe that inclusion is the only way to go. All the kids learn much more. The special needs learners learn in a more inclusive way and they're much happier and more motivated.

(Kelly – learning support facilitator in a mainstream school)

Jonathon is 17 now and he has cerebral palsy. He was in a mainstream setting throughout his schooling and we did all sorts of therapies to try and overcome his motor co-ordination problems. After one operation, he walked for a while but then the stiffness returned and he is now a wheelchair user. When he was 14 he started resisting the attempts to be "normal" and, through one of the groups he attended, developed a pride in who he is – including his disabilities. I am glad that he had the mainstream input as I think that that gave him the strength of character to make the decisions that he now has. He has chosen to live in an adult community with others who are disabled and proud to be so.

(Sue – parent)

in turn gain of ourselves and our place in society. If the perceptions of society about children with disabilities are positive and if special needs are catered for by the child being included completely in all activities, then a positive cycle of growth for the individual as well as the larger community can be enabled.

Internationally, legislation and regulations have worked towards maintaining the special school system, as opposed to providing the same facilities within mainstream schools. This in turn has had the effect of children with special needs being seen as a marginalised group, as not deserving the same as their mainstream peers.

At the same time, in South Africa, this special schooling provision has been segregated and has only provided for a small percentage of children, while the majority of those with disabilities received inadequate or no provision at all. With a new education system that is based on a culture of human rights and thus should promote equal access to inclusive schooling, there is hope that this will change. Of course, as parents, we cannot wait for the changes, but need to act now to educate our children.

CHAPTER 4
CHOOSING AN INCLUSIVE MAINSTREAM SCHOOL

Choosing a school for any child can be difficult. For many children, it may be the first major move away from home and it will be a daily influence for some years ahead. Parents may want a school that will represent their own values and beliefs, and hope that it will be a place for their children to realise dreams, establish close relationships and learn skills and knowledge.

To factor a disability into this equation can make the search for a school an even more daunting task. With the option of mainstreaming being a reality now, the choices that parents are faced with are even greater than before. While this is positive, it can make the task more difficult, and parents are likely to continually question whether the choice made was the best one.

My daughter, Jessica, spent three years in a special school where a specialised method of physical treatment was used. Overall, the time was happy, although I always felt that there were huge demands on such young children – not because of the physical programme, but because they had to "sit and wait" a lot and missed out on the play that is so important for young children.

Jessica then moved to a mainstream school where she has blossomed socially and academically. She is much happier but, on the other hand, she has not been learning as many physical skills. I worry that her physical input is neglected, and I am not sure how to achieve that balance. I often wonder, though, if the pressure to acquire physical skills has come from the society we live in – if society was more accommodating and accessible, would the physical skills really be as necessary?

Accessibility

The way the school provides for both *physical access* and *access to the curriculum* is crucial in your choice of school.

You will need to look at the kind of physical access there is to the school, the classrooms, toilets and the playground. Any physical changes necessary will depend on the school and, of course, your child's needs. Some of these changes could include ramps, handrails, lifts, wide doorways, textured surfaces, switches at accessible heights and accessible toilet facilities.

> My son's school has stairs and we have been able to put in an inexpensive chair lift to get him up to his classroom.
>
> *(Marion – mother)*

> At one time, a learner who had been with us since kindergarten had surgery on her back and, due to a doctor's error, she ended up a paraplegic. They had a great deal of difficulty motivating her. She just gave up. She didn't want to eat or even get out of bed. We felt it would be to her benefit to be amongst her friends and teachers. So we moved her classroom from the second floor to the first floor. When she had to go up or down stairs, then the principal would carry her.
>
> *(Paula – special needs teacher in a mainstream school)*

Physical access to a school often becomes the key focus in a parent's choice of school, but if the details of physical accessibility are foremost in your thinking, then they may be used as an excuse to exclude children. Paula, a special needs teacher in a mainstream school, explains: "Our school is not completely accessible physically, since it's an old building. We tried to remodel it a couple of years ago to make it wheelchair accessible, but we couldn't do it and meet the fire code. So we don't have any children in wheelchairs." Stories like this are familiar. Many buildings are old and many have no wheelchair access. It can be expensive for these things to change and it is exhausting for parents to challenge the system. However, in many schools and universities, it has been achieved and, in some cases, with less cost than initially thought. Bear in mind that there is *always* a way round physical obstacles!

For a mainstream school to include every child entirely, there must be equal *access to the curriculum*, that is, access to all learning opportunities for all children. This may mean:

❖ modifications to provide sensory and communication access; if a child has a visual impairment, then aside from learning to read using Braille, they may need materials presented with far more sensory input – textured materials, bright or shiny paper, contrasting backgrounds or more auditory material

❖ modification of classroom learning activities to ensure that children with special needs can participate, taking their strengths and weaknesses into account

❖ modifications in areas like physical education and extra-mural activities, which are often overlooked; sports equipment and apparatus may, for example, need to be modified

Depending on the needs of your child, you will need to look at access in terms of auditory, visual and communication opportunities. How exactly do children with varied needs access the curriculum? What must be closely examined is just how each child is catered for. More importantly, you need to ascertain whether there is a willingness to make necessary modifications, and whether there is knowledge about which agencies can be approached for guidance and support. Often, things will not be in place until the child is actually attending the school.

If the mainstream school does not see to these access needs of the individual, then it is not genuinely providing access and being inclusive. The stories on this and the next page are examples of schools providing more than just physical access.

> Don't ignore intellectual access. This is far more important than physical access, and it is often overlooked. Children need to be able to access the curriculum and we need to find ways for them to express themselves and make their needs known.
>
> *(James – special needs co-ordinator in a mainstream school)*

> We had a child in Grade 7 with Down's syndrome who was functioning at the level of a six- or seven-year-old. When his class was working on a project, he would draw pictures of the subject, and he learned some of the vocabulary. He loved being able to contribute with the rest of the class, and enjoyed giving his presentation with them as well. The other children helped him to access as much as possible.
>
> *(Cath – teacher in a mainstream school)*

> Ben needs a lot of encouragement to participate, but we can usually keep his attention if we involve him in things like the making of home-made play dough. We then would use the dough as a follow-up to our language activities. So if we were doing nursery rhymes, we might make the characters out of the play dough. We also do a lot of art with him – tracing, painting and sometimes colouring, although he's not crazy about it.
>
> *(Debbie – learning support facilitator in a mainstream school)*

Vincent has perceptual problems, his vision is impaired and he has some cognitive difficulties. I enlarge his worksheets, and we use bright felt pens on contrasting papers, as well as any different materials that I can lay my hands on. If you are imaginative, you can find all kinds of interesting ways to present things to him, and that helps him to learn.

(Marion – learning support facilitator in a mainstream school)

Alice has cerebral palsy, but she is mobile and so can join in with some activities like running or skipping. She has a cast on right now, so she sometimes trips and falls. She loves to participate and always wants to do what the other kids are doing.

(Matt – teacher in a mainstream school)

I have physio at school and at first it was planned to be during my PE lesson. I don't like missing PE because that is one of my favourite subjects. I can join in all the races in my electric wheelchair and when we do ball activities, my friends help me. So now I have physio before school. It means getting up very early on those days, but I prefer it.

(Jessica – age 8)

I have a child with autism in my class. First thing in the morning, we have a discussion and share news. Then we work on sounds or Maths skills. We do these activities together at tables. This works well because the child with autism requires a bit more structure. The class would then have free time followed by snack time, which is outdoors when the weather is fine. The little girl with autism doesn't cope very well with this, but we are trying it to get her used to going outside as that is what will happen next year.

(Sheena – teacher in a mainstream school)

The programme of learning carried out by the teacher should take into account physical access and access to the curriculum, and particular classroom arrangements, especially seating, will depend on the needs of individual children:

❖ children who are visually impaired will need to have a lot of equipment for their Braille; they may not be able to be right in the centre of the class because there may be the need for electric plugs

❖ children who are hearing impaired may benefit from classrooms with carpets because that cuts down on the amount of noise, which is especially important when they're wearing a hearing aid since everything is amplified

❖ if children are easily distracted or have difficulty concentrating, their seating will need to be looked at very carefully; sometimes they need to be at the front, or sometimes they need to be near the teacher; often, they need to have a special workplace within the classroom where a learning support facilitator can work with them more on a one-to-one basis

❖ wheelchairs may be awkward if space is at a minimum and thought will be required in positioning tables; children with walking frames or who have difficulty with mobility or spatial awareness will also need thought given to where they sit in the classroom

Usually when a programme of learning works well for the whole class, it also works well for children with special needs, and it doesn't single them out and make them feel really different. So when schools and teachers can design something that is appropriate for the class and for the individual, everyone gains.

Having fun at the school disco

Attitudes

Attitudes towards inclusion vary from school to school, and often depend on the general ethos of the school. When visiting a mainstream school you are considering for your child, it is helpful to raise contentious issues in order to gauge the general philosophies and views of all those present at the school. Find out:

❖ about other children with disabilities in the school and ask questions about how various situations, like bullying, are dealt with

> Inclusive education may be a new term, but it's an old practice. I feel very good with what happens in our school. Everyone is very accepting, and the goal is the individual child. The questions you hear are "What can we do? How far can we take this child? Where can we go with their learning?"
>
> *(Dianne – teacher in a mainstream school)*

> Initially there was a lot of resistance from teachers about inclusion. Some teachers agreed to have learners with special needs while others would not. So I kind of forced the issue by making everyone accept learners with special needs. I think because I believed in it so strongly, I sold the concept to all. Now the staff have no qualms about taking learners with special needs. It also helped when they realised that they were going to get my support.
>
> *(Di – head of department in a mainstream school)*

> The first step is to listen and to acknowledge that the situation can be stressful. That then opens the doors to working out strategies to deal with the child.
>
> *(Stephanie – special needs teacher in a mainstream school)*

> Our principal is great on encouragement. There is a lot of communication between the teachers and the principal, so if children deserve applause, she will come into the class to congratulate that learner. She also helps with special rewards and lets children do things like make the announcements using the intercom.
>
> *(Beth – teacher in a mainstream school)*

> Most teachers have had good success, even if they had difficulty with the concept of inclusion at the beginning. They find out that it's not as hard as they thought it might be, and it really does work if the support is there.
>
> *(Di – head of department in a mainstream school)*

❖ how "differences" in general are looked upon as this will be a good yardstick with which to gauge attitudes towards disability

❖ how much awareness there is in the school about different disabilities and whether there is knowledge on how to access information if necessary; this will give an indication of how willing the staff are to learn, put policy into practice and be open to new ideas

❖ about the involvement of the governing body of the school, and what interest there is in including all children

Staff's attitudes

It is important for teachers to have the needs of all of their learners as their prime focus. They need to have support in designing an academic programme to suit special needs children. Of course, in classes of 40–60 children, this may seem impossible, but it can be managed with teamwork. In South Africa, it is still uncommon to use the skills of parents or other older family members alongside teachers, and perhaps we can learn from others regarding this notion. In the United Kingdom, parents are called on to help wherever possible – listening to children reading, putting up work on the walls or working with groups of children. It is useful to speak to the school about the kind of support that they can access, and how supported they feel in their situations. Also find out how open they are to calling on support from parents and other family members.

Find out how staff members cope with children's attitudes, how they feel about having class discussions about disability and differences, and which situations they feel need to be explained to children with special needs. Many schools have found that extra information only needs to be given to children where it is necessary and that, in most instances, children will ask questions if they are interested or curious.

Children's attitudes

The children's attitudes are often the most telling, and it is very useful to chat to them incidentally while visiting the playground. It is also interesting to see how they react to other children.

Trying out a friend's wheelchair

> Well, when we started out including children with special needs, we involved everyone in a lot of discussion. As time went on, we found that it's not always necessary. Children are very accepting and they're also really good at figuring things out for themselves. When teachers behave like this is just normal day-to-day stuff, then the children feel that way too and do the same. If there are a lot of questions, we initiate some discussion. Otherwise, a simple conversation or getting children to work with and get to know the child seems to work.
>
> *(Paula – special needs teacher in a mainstream school)*

> Our inclusion policy has been going on for some time and in our school there are at least 15 children with special needs. Most classes have a learner with special needs, and there is a lot of familiarity from playing in the playground. There are times when we will give extra information, or involve the class's support, like if they need to learn a communication system, or some particular behavioural skills. That way the children have specific ways of relating and interacting.
>
> *(Sheena – teacher in a mainstream school)*

> When we visited the school, the special needs co-ordinator took us out into the playground. He said that the kids are long beyond the "staring stage", and that children were more likely to come and ask what class Jessica would be in. Sure enough, this little guy, Logan, broke away from his football game and ran up. His first question – to Jessica – was "what's your name?" and his second was "what class will you be in?". As he ran back to his game, he shouted "cool wheelchair". That was all wonderfully reassuring.
>
> *(Bev – parent)*

Find out how the children are encouraged to challenge stereotypical viewpoints on differences. Ask to see the school policies on things like bullying – this can be telling.

Parents' attitudes

The parents of other children in mainstream schools may sometimes present a challenge. Their attitudes are sometimes the most difficult to change, being the products of previous generations of bias. It takes time and energy for changes in attitude to filter through, and these parents often do not have the benefit of hands-on experience with children with special needs.

> When Michaela first moved into a mainstream school I was worried about what the other parents would say. She can be disruptive and I thought that they would be concerned about how that would affect their children. Her facilitator has been brilliant. Once he got to know her, he could sense when she was going to be difficult. At first he would remove Michaela – take her on an errand, or something to distract her. Then he tried using other children for a group activity and that has worked well. Not only does it calm Michaela and get her to join in, but it has helped the other children to bond with her, accept her, and now they include her more in their games.
>
> *(Andrea – parent)*

Some schools have implemented awareness programmes for parents, and schools that have good communication links with parents generally are those that have the most success in breaking down stereotypes. Many enlist the help of parents for all sorts of activities, and this not only empowers parents, but also helps to build awareness. Knowledge makes it easier to eradicate fear and, in turn, this helps to challenge prejudice.

Policies

It is crucial that the principal and governing body totally support inclusion, as this will greatly affect whether or not it is effective. If the principal truly believes in inclusion then this can only influence the staff in a positive way.

> Behaviour problems are, for the most part, ways of communicating that are not appropriate. I've found that difficult behaviour lessens when you put children in a busy classroom so that they are not bored. If you have them totally involved in interesting activity, they don't have time for a lot of the previously exhibited behaviour. You just have to get them as immersed as possible with their peers.
>
> *(Cath – teacher in a mainstream school)*

Behaviour management

It is very important to find out what the school's behaviour management policies are. Three of the most used strategies are *rewards*, *time-out* and *ignoring behaviour*. If these are not standard practices at the school you are considering, find out what strategies are used particularly with children who are disruptive.

Paula, a special needs teacher in a mainstream school, explains her view on disruptive behaviour: "Often, children who are developmentally delayed exhibit immature behaviour. It's just something that you would see in a younger child, but it's not appropriate at that age. I try to help teachers to see that and realise that it's not such aberrant behaviour, it's just very young behaviour."

> I use fairly standard behaviour management strategies. I aim to maximise the positive, and minimise the negative. I use parent support to set up goals which can be rewarded at home. I also use behaviour charts in the classroom and time-outs if I need to.
>
> *(Matt – teacher in a mainstream school)*

Communication links

Communication links with families are crucial for the ongoing development of the child. It is important to find out what policy about communication with the children's families exist in the school. Is there an open attitude to parents coming in to school to help in the classroom, to talk to the teacher or to other staff, or just to be there as a support? Are there regular meetings set up to encourage communication? Are there home–school diaries for daily communications?

The more that staff know about individual children, the more understanding and awareness there will be, and therefore the more potential for growth on every level. For example, when Jessica's class went on a visit to the Science museum, I went along to help. In the "hands-on" areas, I got Jessica out of her chair to participate with the other children, and, during lunch break, I sat her on the floor with her friends. Her teacher commented afterwards at the surprise it had been to her. She didn't know that Jessica could sit cross-legged, and said: "to see her sitting with the others, where she looked just like one of them, made me realise how when she is up there in her chair, away from them, how 'different' she is". Incidents like these may seem small and trivial, but they show how experiences that give awareness of someone's ability can open the doors to greater learning for everyone.

Find out about staff meetings that are held at the school. Many schools have weekly whole staff meetings and also set aside time for smaller groups to meet. It is important that the staff involved with individual children get a chance to discuss individual children's progress and make any necessary modifications to the learning programme.

Evaluation

Schools should have some method of measuring each child's progress toward annual goals, and monitor whether progress is sufficient to enable children to achieve the goals by the end of the year.

> In terms of tests, we often specify it to the child. We try to develop tests on each topic, but sometimes more specific, and often with fewer questions. We really help the learner to prepare. The facilitator might sit during the test, often scribing the answers if there are difficulties with writing.
>
> *(Paula – special needs teacher in a mainstream school)*

Find out what methods of evaluation are used in the school. This will depend to some extent on how the national outcomes-based education (OBE) curriculum is being implemented. According to the curriculum policy documents, "the new outcomes-based approach has taken the requirements of learners with special education needs into account in the process of developing learning programme guidelines. For learners who experience problems with the basic functions of reading, spelling, writing and calculations, alternative means of assessing will be provided to evaluate their true potential and level of knowledge. The focus on demonstrations and alternative assessment methods, varying from complete exemption from all reading or writing inputs, to partial exemption using tape recorders, amanuenses, etc., bears testimony to this paradigm shift" (October 1997, p. 9).

> We are aware of keeping the self-esteem of all children boosted. We use report cards in our school but keep a check on those of special needs children. We'll only use symbol grading if it is going to be positive for the child. So there might be a child whose Maths or reading is not at the grade level, but they do well in Art or Social Studies. Often we use the term "modified programme" for individual children.
>
> *(Sheena – teacher in a mainstream school)*

Schools should also have some means of regularly informing parents of the child's progress. Most schools send out some sort of report either at the end of each term or bi-annually and these, though individual, often compare the child to the class average. Schools also usually have meetings for parents to look at and discuss their children's work. These are often the most informative ways of viewing the progress a child is making.

Individual education plans

Every child with special educational needs should have an individual education plan (IEP). This is a plan or strategy for the year, stating the goals and the means of achieving them, and information on transition and standardised testing. IEPs are used in the United Kingdom, the United States of America, Canada, Australia and New Zealand. In South Africa, this method is being used in only a few schools. It is not used as the norm, and many children have not reached the stage of having a statement of their needs drawn up. However, it is advisable for every child to have one in order to identify and meet their needs. Not only does it benefit the individual child, but it helps the teacher plan for the year.

It is a great ideal to strive for, and therefore it may be useful to understand how IEPs work. The IEP would usually be a formal document, copies of which reside with the Education Department and with the school. They are set up by a team consisting of the regular classroom teacher and any support staff, like the facilitator, physiotherapist, occupational and/or speech therapist, as well as the parents/carers and the child. The team reviews the IEP yearly, with targets achieved being acknowledged, and further goals set. The team can rewrite the original IEP or submit an amendment, if necessary. Changes to the contents of an IEP, placement of a child, type and hours of related services, and/or hours of special education are usually only made following an IEP meeting.

You should be clear about your level of involvement in the setting of the IEP, and in establishing what individual needs your child has and how they can be catered for by the school. If the school you choose uses IEPs, find out how the school views your level involvement by checking if you can initiate an IEP meeting, if it will be scheduled to include all appropriate school staff, if the school is required to give you notice when it schedules an IEP meeting and, if so, how much. Usually you can invite anyone you want to an IEP meeting – a family member, friend or someone supportive who knows the child and what you want for him or her. You should try never to go alone.

You have the right to and *should* keep a copy of every document the school has on your child. All IEPs, requests and approval for testing, evaluations, etc., should be part of a permanent file you keep on your child.

> In our school, the people who work on the IEPs would be the parents, the classroom teacher and me. We would also invite resource people who work with the child. For example, if the child is visually impaired, then we would have a resource person for the visually impaired. If the child has a pervasive developmental disorder, then the resource person who works with autistic children would help us.
>
> *(Paula – special needs teacher in a mainstream school)*

> Our IEPs for children with special needs are designed completely on an individual basis. There isn't one thing that works with all children, and we have to keep in mind we need to teach to the child and to the ability. We focus on what they can do rather than the disability, where they are and what reasonable goals are.
>
> *(Cath – teacher in a mainstream school)*

> We also have case conferences which can be requested by the teacher, the parents, the school-based team or anyone who is providing services to that child. Case conferences are always held at the beginning of the year when the IEPs are being put together, and then we do a review at least once a year.
>
> *(Matt – teacher in a mainstream school)*

Language

Language is a very powerful yet subtle tool that can undermine or raise the status of something quite dramatically. The most extensive way that views and messages are reinforced is through the use of language, which helps to influence the attitudes of those listening and reflects the attitudes of the speaker.

Because our society sets the norm around able-bodied behaviour, language tends to reflect and reinforce this. It therefore supports and in fact can create a negative image of those with disabilities. Sayings such as "lost your tongue", "it's there, can't you see?", "are you blind?" and "stand up for yourself" permeate the English language. These all sustain the image of disability as negative and encourage an inappropriate and unfair use of labelling. Contrast the images in your mind when you hear the terms "wheelchair bound" and "wheelchair user". Which creates the more independent picture?

Although labels can be useful for describing a medical condition in order that we then know how to provide appropriately for those needs, we need to be aware of the dangers when using labels when it comes to education. Children tend to live up to the expectations of their peers, their teachers and their labels. We need to ensure that their "whole self" is not defined by the label given to their disability. Children have many attributes and this should be kept in mind by all who work with them. This way, the child gets the chance to develop a positive self-image, free of the belief that difficulties are due to a personal flaw or lack of effort and so, too, deep emotional and psychological problems are prevented from developing later.

Find out what the policy is at school on name calling, or referring to disabilities or impairments negatively. If there is no policy, you could set one up. There is plenty of advice available on the way policies should be drafted and what should be included.

Support

Many schools use different ways of encouraging friendships between children, but it is necessary for you to establish whether or not this is a priority in the school you choose. *Monitors/helpers*, *buddies* and *circles of friends* are all different ways of getting children to interact with one another. The roles of peers may range from helping children to get around, helping with elements of school work, getting things ready for work, helping at snack time, to calling staff if needed. All of these things build an awareness of the different needs of people, and hopefully creates compassion for others.

Monitors/helpers are usually children chosen to support specific children with special needs and see to particular things, for example, pushing a wheelchair around in the playground, or opening a book ready for writing. They are often chosen by the child with the special needs and can lead to close bonds of friendship.

> There are two monitors chosen each day to help me and David and Victor. They come in the lift with us, come to the dining hall and help us with our coats. They also call one of the teachers if I need to go to the toilet.
>
> *(Jessica – age 8)*

The *buddy system* has been used in schools in Britain and North America where specific children are nominated to be watchful for those who may be isolated in any way. Children who are feeling left out may approach *buddies* who will then look for ways to make them feel included with their peer groups. This has been found to promote friendship and co-operation in the playground.

> I love being chosen as a monitor. It means we get to go in the lift and at the end of playtime we don't have to line up with the other children but we go up the ramp to the main entrance. We also get to go on the bus on outings and not on public transport.
>
> *(Sam – age 7)*

The concept of *circles of friends* developed in Canada but is now used extensively as a means of developing awareness and compassion in school playgrounds. This concept is based on the idea that people we interact with can be divided into four groups or four "circles of friends": (1) people with whom we have close intimate relationships (like family), (2) people with whom we have close friendships, (3) people with whom we share interests or activities, and (4) people who provide us with certain services (like therapists or social workers). Children in special schools have diminished circles 2 and 3 because they are usually bussed out of their home areas and so have less chances of forming close friendships and, beyond school, have less opportunity to participate in outside interests; whereas those in mainstream schools have the chance to form friendships and are motivated to join other groups. Thus, by mainstreaming children with special needs, there is more opportunity for developing their circles 2 and 3, which in turn opens up possibilities for fulfilling their potential merely through the motivation that is provided through these interactions. By adopting the concept of *circles of friends* as part of the philosophy underlying school policies, the ethos of the school should be one in which empathy and compassion for all are encouraged.

Schools that allow expression of feelings and encourage children to talk really openly with each other seem to create a sense of belonging in the classroom. Differences are recognised and celebrated rather than given negative attention.

Jessica has been assessed as requiring varied support in the classroom. It has been agreed that it is most appropriate for her to have two hours of teacher time with focused help in Maths, and ten hours of assistant time for things like toileting and general help in the classroom.

(Bev – parent)

The facilitators are in the classroom as they are needed. We set up a programme at the beginning of the year, which looks at what my day will be like. We determine where I will need the facilitators' help, and when I think I'll be OK. The facilitators help me modify the curriculum when necessary.

(Cath – teacher in a mainstream school)

The amount of professional support that is available to the child in terms of assistance, therapies and equipment is usually determined by finance, and in South Africa there has historically been huge discrepancies in this kind of provision to different groups of people. It is important that you find out what is available and also what your child is entitled to. These do not always match and you may find that fighting for your child's rights is an ongoing battle. In South Africa, it is often up to parents to provide a learning support facilitator, and of course this can be costly.

Here two teachers in Canadian schools talk about the ways in which they use professional support. Matt is a teacher in a mainstream classroom. He explains: "During the first week, we don't have a facilitator in the class a lot because they want us to kind of get a feel for the class. Besides, we're building a community, and, as the classroom teacher, I feel that when I'm building that community, I need to be the adult in the room. I'm really strong about not having them in my room the first week because I feel that I need to take ownership. The child with special needs has to know that they're a part of my class. That they're a learner in my classroom not because they have a special need, but because they're on my class list and they're a part of the class. I always have the facilitator in the class for the writers' workshop, which is great because not only do they help learners with special needs, but they help all the kids."

Paula is a special needs teacher in a mainstream school. She says: "We have access to any kind of support we need. We have a guidance counsellor who comes in three times a week, as well as psychologists who mostly do the placing and testing of learners. We'll refer to outside agencies if we feel we have a problem that our guidance counsellor cannot handle. There are two different teams. There's a staffing team, which is made up of a psychologist, a social worker, a principal, myself, a speech person, a motor therapist, a para-professional who's working with the learner, the parents, the learner and a peer if we feel that's appropriate. There's also a support team, which is made up of a peer if that's appropriate, the parents, a para-professional, a speech therapist, a motor therapist, the classroom teacher, myself, and anybody else who comes into contact with the learner during the day."

These descriptions from teachers overseas give us something to strive for in order to give our children the quality provision that they deserve. A team approach can be a successful use of resources in that responsibilities are shared. In time, hopefully, South African schools will begin to make use of such strategies. Teachers might share workloads by planning together, or joining classes and team teaching some lessons. For example, having one teacher teach all the reading and the other teach all the Maths while they're both in the classroom at the same time. Another example of sharing teacher resources is to use small-group teaching sessions.

In order to maximise the potential for growth in the individual child, the team needs to work as a whole. Everyone's ideas need to be respected, including those of the child and his or her parents. With schools being increasingly open to sharing ideas, your views as a parent should be welcomed and appreciated.

Transitions

Find out how your chosen school deals with transitions – within the school from class to class, and then on to high school. Often there are formal programmes in place, which can be useful. A visit to the next class to meet the teacher, to get acquainted with the classroom, new toilets, and so on, is reassuring for any child – not just those with special needs. A visit from the high school teachers, or a trip to the new school, can go a long way in allaying fears. It is not only children that gain from this reassurance. It is useful for the next grade teacher to know the new children, to have an idea of their needs, and to be aware of interventions that have been used or programmes that are in place.

> We had a learner with cerebral palsy join our school this year. The classroom teacher and the parents met with the team that was involved with her at the last school. We looked at the facilities and the programmes that they had there, and then we met as a team to plan our own strategy. We met Bronwyn in her class on the first day and introduced her to everyone. Then two other learners showed her around the school.
>
> *(Di – principal of a mainstream school)*

> We have a visually impaired child who will be leaving this year to go into high school. For the last few months, we have had her visit the high school at various times during the day. She has had a chance to become acclimatised to the school at the times that may be the most problematic. Initially she went with a group of peers to visit, and then they went at break time. Now we are trying the time when there may be commotion in the passage ways, and she will try getting through the passages unescorted.
>
> *(Paula – special needs teacher in a mainstream school)*

CHECKLIST

Accessibility

- Is there physical access to the building?
- How do blind children access the curriculum?
- Is every child given equal access to every experience?
- How flexible are the teachers at making modifications where necessary?
- Are the classrooms set up to facilitate co-operative learning?
- Is thought given to the way seating is arranged to facilitate specific children's needs?

Attitudes

- What are the attitudes of the staff towards having children with disabilities in their school?
- How much awareness is there of different disabilities?
- Does the governing body of the school show an interest in including all children?
- How are the children encouraged to challenge stereotypical viewpoints on differences?
- To what extent are parents encouraged to be involved in school activities?

Policies

- How does the governing body of the school view policies on special needs?
- Is the school open to parents being involved in decision making?
- Does the school have policies on:
  - behaviour management
  - communication links between parents and staff, and staff and other people with whom children with special needs have contact
  - evaluation
  - language
  - support for children with special needs
  - transitions from class to class or from primary to secondary school?

CHAPTER 5
GETTING GOING

The society that we live in has strongly entrenched biases and children with special needs are likely to suffer the prejudices of those with stereotyped views. In time, we hope that these will be challenged and will change with understanding and awareness, but right now our children and families are the teachers initiating these shifts.

Preparing your child

Children's learning experiences in the early years will help them to form self-concepts, and these need to be as strong and positive as possible. As they grow older, they will hopefully build on these skills to become as independent and self-sufficient as they possibly can.

The first thing that we can do as parents is to recognise the widespread bias that permeates the society we live in. With this awareness, you will realise how the subtle but constant messages give perpetual reinforcement to negative views on disability. Unless we begin to shift these and take some active stand, we promote and support them by our silence. We need to counteract the stereotypes that pervade our lives in advertising, on TV and in the community at large. We need to challenge those in our homes, schools and lives, taking every opportunity to do so. We can do this by providing children with contrasting images to the stereotypical ones that are prevalent.

Language is a communication tool, and the greater your child's grasp, the more powerful the use. To start school with the ability to express their needs is an advantage to all children. You as a parent can take every opportunity to build your child's language. It is important to understand the crucial role of language, so that every possible chance to develop language is taken up. Some of the following can be used as guidelines:

❖ listen to your children and let them feel that you value what they say

❖ if your children do not speak, give them time to communicate in whatever way they can, for example, using Bliss symbolics, or a Rebus pointer

❖ draw your children into everyday discussions and plans

❖ make time to talk about feelings – yours and theirs

❖ talk to your children about things that interest them

❖ join a library and visit regularly with your children

❖ if there is a storytime at the library, encourage them to listen

❖ read to them

❖ listen to them read, or look at books together

❖ show them that you enjoy reading by letting them see you read

❖ choose books that reflect diverse images that will counteract biases

❖ use every opportunity to create scrapbooks, journals, notes and drawings for your children to document any experience

Children need to be as independent as possible, but learning lifeskills is a gradual process. However, you can encourage this process by using some of the ideas in the following list. Even if your children have limited function, you can involve them in activities, and the more that is done in their early years, the more they (and you) will benefit later on:

❖ encourage your children to do as much alone as possible in toileting, dressing and feeding skills

❖ involve them in as many household activities as you can – preparing food, laying the table, cleaning and tidying

❖ include them in outdoor activities, for example, gardening

❖ teach them about means of getting around – catching buses/trains/taxis

❖ show them how to tell the time

❖ help them to write letters or cards

❖ teach them to answer the phone, make calls and take messages

❖ help them to recognise stereotypes

❖ encourage them to challenge biased behaviour

❖ if they use discriminatory behaviour, challenge this in a caring way and build an awareness of "fair" and "unfair" practices

❖ teach them to negotiate with others

❖ teach them to thank others for help when it is offered, and how to assert themselves when the help offered is not the kind needed

Feelings are not always given the degree of importance that they deserve. Right from the start, children need to be in touch with the way they are feeling, and they need to be given the language to express this. They should hear words like happy, excited, angry, sad and frustrated from the early days when they are having their nappies changed. Then, as they begin to speak, they will be able to use the words to express these feelings. If they never speak, they will still understand these words and use them in whatever method of communication they develop. Even if children are given the language but cannot verbalise it, the frustrations will be reduced, just knowing that someone is taking the time to express it for them. This will also contribute a tremendous amount towards making them feel valued.

Here are some ways of supporting your children's emotional development:

* learn to recognise what your children are feeling, and give appropriate language, for example, "I can see how angry you are feeling" or "you are excited this morning"

* use opportunities to build positive self-identity; draw attention to the positive things about your children, for example, the way they look and the things they can do

* explore the difference between feelings of superiority and pride in oneself; to develop a positive self-esteem does not mean that one has to adopt a superior attitude

* give yourself the chance to become aware of the way you feel about your children's disabilities and the way stereotypes in society influence this

* look at the way images of disability in your culture can be either fair and true, or not; how do the unfair or untrue representations make you feel? how do they make your child feel?

* foster an environment of diversity and show your children the value of this

* give them the opportunity to meet others with similar disabilities

* respect and value your children's feelings

* listen to and answer questions directly and truthfully; listen to the expression of feelings in the questions too

* encourage your children to express themselves freely and in ways that are appropriate for them but that do not impinge on the rights of others

* initiate discussions about positive role models – people that you or your children can identify with, of whom you feel proud

In order for your children to be active participants in their community, they need to be able to socialise in confident and assertive ways. They need to feel safe, accepted and supported. They need to feel a sense of belonging. In order to achieve this, they will need to grow up in a community where these principles are nurtured. With the change in family structures and the pressures that our societies often present, it is a challenge to ensure this for our children. There is particular pressure on parents with children who have disabilities. The families are often isolated at the very time that they need the most support. Without practical support, the family and the child will flounder, and without emotional support, anger and resentment can build up, with detrimental effects on the child and the rest of the family. Outside the immediate family, the school and the network that it provides can be an extended support. Do not be afraid to take up any opportunities of help and support – both physical and emotional.

All of the above suggestions would be useful to employ with any child. All children need to be able to recognise and express feelings, to master and be competent users of their own language, to enjoy books, to play constructively and to interact positively in a social situation. All children need to have a good self-image and a compassionate understanding of people who are different to them in some way. However, children with disabilities or, for that matter, any "difference" are likely to have to work harder to achieve, fit in or be accepted in the mainstream environment. Not only do they have to deal with whatever specific problems they have, but they have to overcome the negative perceptions that abound.

By giving the children every opportunity to develop a healthy self-esteem, the only thing left in order that they go off to school in a confident and prepared manner is to do what any parent should do – give them an awareness and an understanding of school life. You can do this by doing the following:

❖ look at books about starting school, or starting a new school

❖ attend the open day visits before the term begins

❖ if there is a uniform, involve your child in buying it, putting name labels on it, and have it all ready

❖ have your child involved with getting all the other school things together – school bag, pencils, etc.

❖ talk about what may happen on the first day

❖ get friendly with some of the other children likely to be in the same class or beginning at the same time

Preparing the school

Work will be required in the school, and, as a parent, you have a vested interest. If the school of your choice is open to suggestions, you may be able to get fully involved in the development of inclusion. If the school does not have one, they will need to develop a "whole school" policy and they may need help in doing this, particularly if funds and resources are at a premium.

Although it may seem a daunting task, many parents have been the initiators behind schools developing inclusion policies and accepting children with a range of disabilities. It takes great energy and the battle can be long and difficult, but it can and has been done. Groups and individuals from the United Kingdom, the United States of America and Canada have been involved in research and in setting up inclusion projects in southern Africa. These and other organisations in South Africa can be contacted for literature and advice. Refer to the Useful Contacts section on page 53 for a list of organisations that may be able to assist you. Many therapists and private consultants are also willing to accompany parents to schools. Also other parents can be of valuable support and encouragement. Knowledge is a powerful tool and you will benefit from approaching the available associations and resources for literature and information.

Resources will need managing. As a parent, you may have information about your child's special needs or related advice that could resource the school, or you may be in a position to help with gathering information. You may have, or have access to, resource packs with up-to-date information, which will instruct or enlighten staff, other parents or children. You may have contact with specific organisations that can send information, arrange workshops or act in an advisory capacity.

The curriculum will need development. According to current policy, this responsibility belongs to the school governing body and the staff. However, in reality, there may be the need for more parent involvement at least in the initial stages. Ensuring that learners with disabilities have access to every facet of school life will need development and monitoring. Here are some areas in which you, as parent, could offer advice and assistance:

- sensory and communication access
- sports equipment and apparatus
- ramps
- rails
- doors – wide doorways, glass panels, etc.
- toilets
- playground
- lifts (where necessary)
- textured surfaces
- switches at heights accessible to all

Staff development is another area that will need examining, and, again, there may be the need for some parental involvement. Areas that will need to be examined include:

❖ roles and responsibilities of key staff

❖ calling on expertise in special schools or at other institutions

❖ bridges between mainstream and special schools

❖ classroom visits by professionals

❖ workshops to build awareness for staff as well as children and other parents

For your child to be included fully, the development of the other children at the school is another area that will require work. Although the staff and the governing body of the school will be responsible for this in policy, the reality is that parents have much to offer. You may be able to help with or advise on many of the following aspects:

❖ building awareness of disabilities: physical, mental and emotional barriers

❖ challenging stereotypes

❖ creating awareness of negative language and building positive language instead

Even if the school is becoming an inclusive environment, all of the above issues will need monitoring and, as parents, we need to be aware of the constant need for reassessment of the issues. For the benefit of your child and any that will follow, your guidance and assistance cannot be underestimated. You may not want to be an activist, but, through your experiences with your child, you are in a knowledgeable position.

> I want any advice that people can give me. I want the parents with their opinions, any professional's views, and the best thing is really listening to the child. If they do not speak, you have to "listen" very carefully, but they will let you know how best to handle them.
>
> *(Paula – special needs teacher in a mainstream school)*

Schools and teachers need to have adequate background knowledge and advice in order to help your child to develop his or her full potential, which is where your contributions are needed. From seating arrangements to eating methods, you may be able to provide tips that will make things easier for the staff, and this in turn may lead to your child progressing steadily.

Preparing yourself

The more informed you are, the more prepared you will feel. Get as much information as possible on:

❖ your rights

❖ the Department of Education's policies for learners with disabilities

❖ the school and its inclusion policy

Be assertive in your dealings with the school and with any other professionals. This means:

❖ expressing your needs clearly and directly

❖ communicating effectively with your child, the school and any professionals

❖ feeling confident about ensuring that your child gets what he or she rightfully deserves

❖ conveying your self-confidence by stating what you need and want

❖ expressing your ideas without feeling guilty or intimidated

❖ standing up for what you believe your child needs – even though professionals may not agree – but also remaining open to other possibilities

❖ developing professional relationships

❖ knowing your rights and how to establish them (not leaving things to others because you feel they may know better)

❖ documenting your child's needs

❖ advocating effectively on behalf of your own child

❖ only acting when you have all of the facts

❖ persisting until you get all the services your child needs

❖ analysing a problem and pinpointing areas of responsibility before you act

❖ agitating to get necessary legislation passed and implemented

❖ organising for change, that is, not acting only on your own behalf and for your child, but also for those who follow or who have similar needs

Here are some suggestions that may help you to help your child:

❖ keep your child as much in the mainstream of your community as possible

❖ do all that you would with your child if there was no disability, like join various playgroups, go swimming or visit the library

- ❖ apply to register your child in the pre-school, primary or secondary school of your choice
- ❖ allow your child to participate in group activities with children of the same age
- ❖ invite peers home to play or, when they are older, have sleep-overs
- ❖ find support groups as well (although mainstream may be the focus, in order to survive it, it is important to have groups to identify with and to support you and your child)

It can be difficult to find ways to ensure that your child gets equal opportunities to socialise in the same way that peers are doing. It is often emotionally draining to be continually challenging the social system in order to allow your child appropriate social interaction with same-aged playmates. It is a challenge to be breaking down the stereotypes that these children have learned from their parents, and even more difficult to alter the views of the parents. The best way to do this is to just "hang in there". The more other children and their families are challenged, the more quickly opinions will change, though it is tiring to be constantly the initiator of these changes.

Set up support for yourself in as many ways as possible:

- ❖ a support group of parents with similar needs
- ❖ a support group of parents who are committed to ensuring that diversity is celebrated in our schools
- ❖ a counsellor or a therapist to work through your issues, that is, those to do with your child and the disability, and how it has impacted on your life – perhaps a social worker, or counsellor at a parent's centre or clinic
- ❖ a helper (or team of helpers) to give you hands-on assistance and some time off
- ❖ some sort of respite provision so that you get regular breaks, for example, help in the home or a respite care place where the child can visit with another family; in the UK there is a system called *family links* where families take on a child with special needs and have them for one out of every six weekends, for instance
- ❖ a network of friends who will just listen or offer practical support, for example, a friend who helps to mind your child or who will offer to do some cooking

CHAPTER 6
KEEPING GOING

Often when children begin at school, parents feel that the professionals are now the decision makers and in control, and they lose sight of their role in the guidance of their children's lives. It is important to maintain a close link with the school, and at the same time to monitor progress areas that you feel are important.

It is necessary that the child is systematically observed to ensure progression towards the targets that have been set by the team (parent, child, class teacher and any support staff and therapists). Everyone in the team could observe and give input at meetings regarding the child's progression. Make sure that the targets are realistic. It may be useful to draw up a checklist for you as a parent to use in monitoring your child's progress. This could include:

❖ physical progress: What milestones have my child achieved?

❖ academic progress: What areas of the curriculum have improved/need work on?

❖ inclusion: How much does my child participate in mainstream activity?

❖ peer group: What opportunities do I provide for socialising? How is my child's self-esteem?

❖ discipline: What behaviour management strategies are we using?

As your child moves class, as with any child, there will need to be careful planning with the new teacher to ensure a smooth transition. If your child changes schools, the liaison is more necessary in order to maintain a steadiness in the child's progress. The *link* programme that is used between some schools, whereby children from both schools spend time in the other to learn and build awareness, can be a useful exercise.

As a parent, you can do the following in terms of achieving an easy transition:

❖ believe in your child

❖ listen to what your child has to say and make sure your child gives input in transition planning

❖ allow your child to make life choices and then to feel the consequences of the decision

❖ continue to give your child as much social interaction as possible

- ❖ monitor and initiate transition processes through the school and broader social system if necessary
- ❖ ensure that the transition plan is relevant to your child's future needs
- ❖ identify resources that your child may need in the future
- ❖ think ahead to your child's adulthood

CHAPTER 7
CONCLUSION

Jessica has provided me with all sorts of opportunities to learn and to explore. She offers me challenges and allows me to see the world through a perspective of difference. Her determination continues to inspire me, and I hope it will do the same for you.

> Today at school we were talking about feelings and emotions, and Miss Green asked us to think of words that our parents use to describe us. Shannon said that her mother thinks she is shy. I said that my mother calls me determined. I am determined cos I am determined to learn to walk. I want to be like all my friends who can walk. I am determined to prove the doctors wrong about my walking. Last year at school they said I wouldn't be able to write and had to use the computer and I proved

them wrong and learnt to do
joined up writing like everyone
else in my class. I think watching
everyone at school makes me more
determined cos I can see what
they all can do. If I could
walk I could go on the challenge
at playtime whenever I want to.
I could walk to the toilet without
getting an adult to take me.
I could bring you tea in bed and
make you breakfast. I could do
anything. And I am going to!!

USEFUL CONTACTS

In South Africa

Disabled Children Action Group (DICAG)
Cape Town
Tel: (021) 462 4105
Fax: (021) 462 4665

Durban
Tel: (031) 304 3555
Fax: (031) 304 3559
Email: dicag@iafrica.com

Disabled People South Africa (DPSA)
Western Cape
Tel: (021) 465 0090
Fax: (021) 456 0098
Email: dpsa-ct@global.co.za

Eastern Cape
Tel: (043) 743 1579
Fax: (043) 722 9470

KwaZulu-Natal
Tel: (031) 304 3555/8
Fax: (031) 304 3559

Mpumalanga
Tel: (013) 794 1711
Fax: (013) 794 0689

Northern Province
Fax: (015) 303 1656

Gauteng
Tel: (011) 333 4505
Fax: (011) 333 4822

Free State
Tel: (057) 396 5600 or 396 4089
Fax: (057) 396 1722

North West Province
Tel/fax: (018) 381 6554

Disability Unit, University of Cape Town
Tel: (021) 650 3726

Human Rights Commission
Website: www.sahrc.org.za

Western Cape
Tel: (021) 426 2277
Fax: (021) 426 2875
Email: sahrcwp@global.co.za

Eastern Cape
Tel: (041) 582 4094 or 582 2611
Fax: (041) 582 2204
Email: sahrcpe@global.co.za

Northern Province
Tel: (015) 291 3500 or 291 3504
Fax: (015) 291 3505
Email: sahrcbg@global.co.za

KwaZulu-Natal
Tel: (031) 304 7323/4/5
Fax: (031) 304 7323
Email: sahrckzn@global.co.za

Free State
Tel: (051) 447 1130
Fax: (051) 447 1128

Gauteng
Tel: (011) 484 8300
Fax: (011) 484 8403
Email: sahrc@org.za

Western Cape Forum for Inclusive Education
Tel: (021) 674 1422
Fax: (021) 683 6379
Email: included@mweb.co.za

In the United Kingdom

Alliance for Inclusive Education
Tel: + 0207 735 5277
Fax: + 0207 735 3828
Email: ALLFIE@btinternet.com

Centre for Studies on Inclusive Education (CSIE)
Tel: + 0117 923 8450
Fax: + 0117 923 8460
Website: http://inclusion.uwe.ac.uk

Parents for Inclusion
Tel: + 020 7735 7735
Helpline: + 020 7582 5008
Email: info@parentsforinclusion.org
Website: www.parentsforinclusion.org

BIBLIOGRAPHY

Department of Education. (October 1997) *Foundation phase policy document.*

Goosen, M. & Klugman, B. (1996) *The South African women's health book.* Cape Town: Oxford University Press

Leadbetter, J. and Leadbetter, P. (1993) *Special children: meeting the challenge in the primary school.* London: Cassell

Murray, P. and Penman, J. (1996) *Let our children be: a collection of stories.* Sheffield: Parents with Attitude

National Committee for Education Support Services (1997) *Quality education for all: Overcoming barriers to learning and development.* South Africa: Department of Education

Newman, S. (1999) *Small steps forward.* London: Jessica Kingsley

Rieser, R. and Mason, M. (1990) *Disability equality in the classroom: a human rights issue.* London: Inner London Education Authority

UNESCO and the Spanish Ministry of Education and Science (1994) *The Salamanca statement and framework for action on special needs education.*